Camp Confidence

A play

Diana Raffle

A SAMUEL FRENCH ACTING EDITION

SAMUEL FRENCH

FOUNDED 1830

SAMUELFRENCH.COM
SAMUELFRENCH-LONDON.CO.UK

FOR PRODUCTION ENQUIRIES

UNITED STATES AND CANADA

Info@SamuelFrench.com
1-866-598-8449

UNITED KINGDOM AND EUROPE

Plays@SamuelFrench-London.co.uk
020-7255-4302/01

Each title is subject to availability from Samuel French, depending upon country of performance. Please be aware that *CAMP CONFIDENCE* may not be licensed by Samuel French in your territory. Professional and amateur producers should contact the nearest Samuel French office or licensing partner to verify availability.

MUSIC USE NOTE

Licensees are solely responsible for obtaining formal written permission from copyright owners to use copyrighted music in the performance of this play and are strongly cautioned to do so. If no such permission is obtained by the licensee, then the licensee must use only original music that the licensee owns and controls. Licensees are solely responsible and liable for all music clearances and shall indemnify the copyright owners of the play(s) and their licensing agent, Samuel French, against any costs, expenses, losses and liabilities arising from the use of music by licensees. Please contact the appropriate music licensing authority in your territory for the rights to any incidental music.

IMPORTANT BILLING AND CREDIT REQUIREMENTS

If you have obtained performance rights to this title, please refer to your licensing agreement for important billing and credit requirements.

CAMP CONFIDENCE

First presented at the Medway Little Theatre on 26th July 2005
with the following cast:

Julia Nelson	Amy Sinden
Fiona Saddler	Carolyn Hawkes
Maria Gonzalez	Andrea Sloman
Blanche Happ	Jan Hooper
Donna White	Nic Grint
Cherry Gordon	Holly Chittenden
Blanche Smellie	Alison Cox

Directed by Catherine Kenny

CHARACTERS

Julia Nelson: course leader, organized and intelligent; 39
Fiona Saddler: Julia's assistant, terribly nervous, clumsy; 39
Maria Conchita Juanita Gonzalez: emotional, terrified of
  birds, Mexican; 50
Blanche Happ: mild, kindly, agoraphobic; 55
Donna White: unhappy single mum, on probation; 44
Cherry Gordon: an obsessive cleaner; 29
Blanche Smellie: Donna's probation officer; 46

The action of the play takes place in a campsite

Time — the present

Also by Diana Raffle
published by Samuel French

Blue Suede Blues

CAMP CONFIDENCE

An area in a campsite. 1.10 p.m.

There are two or three tents in this area with various items of camping equipment lying around them. Tent A is L, tent B C, with a washing line or airer between them, a peg basket hanging on it. There is a small picnic table, with chairs, to one side

When the play begins the stage is empty

Julia enters, carrying a bag and holding a mobile phone to her ear. She is followed by Fiona, who appears to be a terribly nervous person and who is struggling under the weight of a huge rucksack to which is attached a large plastic tea tray

Julia (*into the phone*) Roger, are you there?
Fiona Is this it?
Julia (*into the phone*) Pick up the phone Roger, it's important.
Fiona (*looking around*) Is this our spot?
Julia (*nodding to Fiona; into the phone*) At last — where have you been?

Fiona looks in the tents

Well, why didn't you use the spare key; you know I always keep one in the squirrel's bottom.

Fiona gives Julia the thumbs-up

I don't care if it was an emergency, Darren should have put it back. ... So where is it now?

Fiona Shall I start unpacking? (*She takes the rucksack off*)
Julia (*putting her hand over the phone; to Fiona*) Yes.

Fiona puts the rucksack down

    (*Into the phone*) No!

Fiona quickly picks the rucksack up again

    Ring Darren up and make him come back. If he was upset enough
to let himself into our house and drink a bottle of vodka, things
must be bad. The last thing we want is for him to be able to let
himself in again, he knows where I hide the cognac. (*Putting her
hand over the phone; to Fiona*) Why don't you put that awful
thing down, Fiona? I'm beginning to feel as though I'm being
followed by a very small, unattractive snail.
Fiona (*putting the rucksack on the ground*) Sorry.
Julia (*into the phone*) No, I've changed my mind. Just pick it up and
make it quick.

*Fiona jumps, grabs the rucksack, throws it over her shoulder and
knocks into Julia, who drops the phone and puts her hand over her
nose*

Fiona Oh goodness, Julia, I'm so sorry ... (*She gets a hankie out and
hands it to Julia*) Here ...
Julia I think you may have broken my nose. (*She holds the hankie
to her nose. Blood appears on the hankie*)
Fiona I'm sorry, it's just you shouted at me and you know how
nervous I get when you shout. Keep your head back.
Julia (*tilting her head back; holding her nose*) Where's my phone?
Fiona I'm so sorry, was it an important call?
Julia I was talking to Roger. My stepson has had yet another fall-
out with his common wife again.
Fiona Don't you mean common-law wife?

Julia Not in this case. (*Reaching her hand out, searching for the phone*) Where the hell is my phone?

Fiona (*finding the phone*) Here it is ... (*She listens to the phone*) Hallo ... Hallo? Oh dear, I think your husband's been discommunicated.

Julia I think you'll find that happened after his first divorce.

Fiona Oops, you're bleeding again. Keep your head back ...

Julia tilts her head back

That's right.

Julia What time is it?

Fiona Quarter past one.

Julia Bloody hell, our clients should have been here fifteen minutes ago. Look, I can't let them see me like this. You're going to have to stall them.

Fiona But I haven't learnt anything about stalling techniques; you only asked me to hand out the welcome drinks.

Julia Well, do that then, just until I can get cleaned up a bit. (*She grabs her bag and goes into one of the tents*)

Fiona Right, OK, I can do that. I just don't want to let you down. I know how hard you worked to get certified.

Julia, on her knees, comes back out of the tent clutching her make-up bag

Julia Qualified, and yes I have worked hard. Evening classes aren't a soft option, you know. It takes stamina to be lectured to by an ageing hippie whose breath could have been marketed as a facial peel. It was just lucky that I have a natural empathy with people so the coursework was more of a formality.

Fiona You always were cleverer than me.

Julia More clever.

Fiona See what I mean.

Julia Look Fiona, when I made you hand in your notice at "Bernie's Bangers", it wasn't so that you could be on the dole within the month. This business is practically guaranteed to work. I've done my research and the new woman wants confidence. That's why we're providing them with a "Confidence Building Weekend".

Fiona Yes, but I'm still not awfully sure that I'm the person to give that to them.

Julia All you have to do is say "hallo" and show them to their tents; it's hardly brain surgery. (*She sits in one of the chairs, produces a compact from her bag and looks into its mirror as she cleans her face with Fiona's handkerchief*) Why don't you run through the questionnaires with me quickly before everyone arrives.

Fiona OK, yes, good idea. Well, first we've got a lady called Blanche who says that she finds going outside difficult, then there's Donna who says that she finds going inside difficult.

Julia I can't see those two striking up an immediate friendship.

Fiona Then we have Cherry. She was the lady who rang twice about the environmental health agency's report on the camp facilities. I told her she should just put a bit of paper round the loo seat if she was really worried.

Julia Right, and who's the fourth lady we're expecting?

Fiona Maria; she's got a thing about birds, especially chickens.

Julia But isn't the camp entertainer wandering around dressed as a chicken?

Fiona I didn't think Chester would count. He's very popular with the campers apparently. Anyway, don't worry because I checked with the manager and Chester is just about to start a half hour musical tribute to Shakin' Stevens in the Themed Brasserie. Maria should be with us by then.

Julia Fantastic! This is supposed to be a "Confidence-Building Weekend"; we'll be lucky if any of them ever get the confidence to reach the tents, let alone join in any of the activities.

Fiona This will be a success, this is a success, we are a success — isn't that what we say?

Julia If any of them ever get the courage to leave the minibus, it might be very useful.

Fiona (*handing the phone to Julia*) Did you want to ring Roger again?

Julia No, it can wait. What about you? Did you say your goodbyes to Rupert, the fastest mincer in the factory?

Fiona He rushed his order of pork and beef just to take me out last night. I couldn't ask for a more perfect man.

Julia Take it from me Fiona, no man is perfect.

Fiona Are you and Roger not happy, then?

Julia Look, Fiona, love is hardly my priority at the moment. I am simply trying to build a business. Then when you and Rupert decide to go out for a romantic supper you will have some wages with which to pay for it. Perhaps you should think about that.

Fiona I'm sorry, I didn't mean anything ...

Julia And just for the record, Roger and I have a great marriage and we eat out all the time.

Fiona Perhaps we could meet up then. How about the new Beefeater?

Julia My husband isn't a steak man — he prefers trout.

Maria enters carrying a bag. She is Mexican

Maria Excuse — please.

Julia Ah hallo, you must be ...

Maria Tar veen.

Fiona gets her papers out of the rucksack and hurriedly looks through them

Julia Tar veen?

Maria No ... Ees tarr veen.

Fiona We don't seem to have anyone of that name on the list ... Are you sure you are in the right place? You have come for the Camp Confidence.

Maria Si ... My name is Maria Conchita Juanita Gonzalez.

Fiona Oh you're Maria.

Maria Si and I'm star-ving.

Julia Oh I see, you're (*drawling*) starving.

Maria Si ... (*Impersonating the way Julia says it*) Staaarving.

Julia Well, as soon as everybody else arrives we shall make our way
to the restaurant. I thought we'd treat ourselves for our first night.
No camp-fire cooking until tomorrow.

Fiona Dinner starts at seven-thirty.

Maria I no go ... I no go if big bird ees steel playing in restaurant.

Julia Big bird?

Fiona I think she means the camp entertainer. The one dressed as
a chicken.

Maria Chicken, yes ... (*She flaps her arms*) He make bad noise —
make me very scared. I no go if he there, OK?

Julia That's fine, Maria, don't you worry. I'm sure we can organize
some sandwiches or something. Now why don't you have a look
in the tent we have allocated to you, and maybe unpack your
rucksack; what do you say?

Maria I no like birds ...

Julia So we heard. Which of these is Miss Gonzalez's tent, Fiona?

Fiona (*checking her list*) Tent A. Here, I'll hold the flap for you.
(*She moves to tent A*)

Maria I no like flap ... Birdies flap ... Big flap flap ... Make my head
go funny ...

Fiona Sorry, I meant door, the tent door. (*She holds the tent door
open*) There you see, it's really quite cosy — isn't it?

*Maria looks suspicious and bends down to go in. She suddenly darts
back up again*

Maria My husband, he likes birds ...

Julia Name a man that doesn't.

Maria He make me pluck birds, ee say I get to like them. All day
I am plucking, my hands they are big and red and all I can see ees
this great bird's eye staring at me, like he knows I am scared, like
he gonna come alive and peck out my eyes. My husband says I am
a stupid plucker.

Julia Surely not.

Maria One day I got so scared I ran from the house ... I was just
crazy, and I ran to the top of the hill above our village, screaming
and crazy: I was just like this ... (*She demonstrates*)

Fiona Oh yes, I see.

Maria My husband, he go mad ... He follow me, he wave this chicken at me and suddenly I go even more crazy.

Julia Even more crazy: who'd have thought it possible, eh?

Maria So I get to top of hill OK — and he come up waving chicken — like theese ... (*She demonstrates*) Then I suddenly look down — and I remember ...

Fiona What?

Maria (*screaming*) *Aieee!* I no like heights.

Julia Oh, for goodness' sake.

Maria He left me one week later — for Carlita; he say she no old and silly, he say she no frightened of nothing.

Fiona Oh how terrible for you. No wonder you felt in the need for Camp Confidence.

Maria You think you can 'elp me?

Fiona I doubt it.

Julia (*interrupting*) Oh, of course we can help you; this course was designed for people with your problems and you mustn't think that you're on your own. I don't know if you realized it but those three ladies who travelled with you on the minibus are just like you.

Maria They like me?

Julia Si ... I mean yes, just like you.

Maria They all silly old pluckers too?

Julia I shouldn't be at all surprised.

Blanche enters with a rucksack, inching her way nervously across the stage towards the tents

Fiona (*to Blanche*) Oh, hallo and welcome to Camp Confidence, I'm Fiona, your camp greeter. (*Reading lines from a sheet*) This is our leader, Julia, who will be helping you to tackle your particular problems during this all-inclusive outdoor confidence-boosting experience.

Blanche nods nervously, still trying to edge towards the tents

Julia (*to Blanche*) Oh, welcome. I'm so glad you made it. You're
   actually the second person to arrive; Maria here only arrived a few
   minutes ago, didn't you Maria?

Maria Si.

Julia Did you have trouble leaving the minibus?

Blanche (*gingerly holding out her hand*) Miss Happ.

Maria You see big bird too?

Blanche No, you don't understand. I'm the Miss Happ.

Fiona You mustn't say that; whatever problems you have, you
   mustn't blame yourself — must she, Julia?

Julia Of course not.

Blanche No, my name is Happ, Blanche Happ. Neither of which
   is at all funny until you address me as Miss.

Julia We do understand, Miss Happ. Now why don't we get you
   settled in?

Blanche Yes, and I would grateful if you could show me to my tent
   quickly ... I don't like being outdoors too long.

Julia Oh, yes, of course, Blanche, you're in tent B. Fiona, show
   Blanche to her tent and open the flaps for her.

Maria You say flaps ... I no like, it remind me of bird. It drive me
   crazy.

Julia Sorry, Maria — we'll call them doors in future shall we? Tent
   doors. See, Fiona's making a note of it now, aren't you, Fiona?

Fiona Am I?

Julia Now Blanche, let's get you settled in. As Fiona said, I'm Julia,
   your team leader. I think we spoke on the phone, didn't we?

Blanche (*kneeling down by one of the tents*) No, you spoke to my
   sister actually; she was the one who booked the weekend, she
   thought it would help us. We both have a bit of a problem with
   going outside, you see.

Maria You have sister?

Blanche Yes, five, actually.

Maria Your papa sure have a lot of mishaps.

Fiona I think it's lovely that you've got a sister and how nice to have
   the same interests; imagine how lonely you'd be if your sister
   liked going out.

Blanche sits in tent B with her head sticking out. Julia and Fiona bend down to either side of her

Blanche You make it sound like a hobby. It's not like that, you know. I haven't been further than the local shop for years and poor Mimi — that's my sister — hasn't even been able to venture into the back garden since 1983.

Fiona Oh, you poor things.

Julia So, is Mimi on her way here now?

Blanche No, I'm afraid, my sister didn't make it.

Fiona Oh, Blanche, I'm so sorry ...

Julia Yes, yes we both are very sorry. It must have been a terrible wrench.

Blanche It was, I had to leave her clinging to the banister. The front door just proved too much in the end.

Julia Oh, I see. Well, I'm sure she'll be pleased that at least one of you made it. And remember, you're not alone here. Just before you arrived we were telling Maria that all of our guests this weekend have fears and phobias. That is exactly what this weekend course is all about, combating those fears with a mixture of confidence and breathing techniques.

Blanche Being outdoors makes me panicky.

Julia That's where my breathing tips can help you.

Maria I had friend, si? She panic ...

Fiona Really?

Maria She walk into middle of road and freeze, just like theese. (*She demonstrates*)

Blanche She panicked?

Maria Si ... she paanicked.

Julia So what happened?

Maria She got run over by a bus.

Julia Thank you, Maria, that was very helpful.

Blanche That's why I don't go out.

Julia I think you'd better put Blanche down for sandwiches, too, Fiona.

Fiona Oh dear, but we've booked the restaurant now.

Julia Well, unless our other two guests have bumped into Paul McKenna on their momentous journey here, I see little chance of us getting as far as the toilets for the weekend.

Blanche I was hoping there'd be a Portaloo. So I didn't have to go too far.

Julia Actually, Blanche, we'd rather you did. It's a good exercise for your sort of phobia. Need overcoming fear. You need to go to the toilet so you are forced to brave the open space between your tent and the cubicles.

Blanche If I get too desperate, sometimes I go in my bag.

Fiona Oh.

Maria I no share tent with Miss Happ who have mishap ...

Julia That's quite enough of that, Blanche, after this weekend I can assure you, you won't be wanting to pee into your handbag again.

Blanche No, I think you've misunderstood me ... I've had a bag fitted to my leg ever since my hysterectomy, you see. I was offered an operation to fix it but I haven't been able to face going to hospital again.

Fiona Oh look. We have another guest arriving.

Maria I definitely no sleep in that tent.

Donna and Cherry enter with their bags

Fiona Make that two! Welcome, welcome, you must be — —

Donna Bloody terrified.

Fiona Of course, and your name is ...?

Donna Donna, Donna White.

Fiona Welcome to Camp Confidence Donna, my name's Fiona and I'm your greeter for today. This is our leader Julia who will be helping you to tackle your particular problems during this all-inclusive outdoor confidence-boosting experience.

Julia Hallo Donna, your journey may have been difficult but let me assure you that you have already come a long way today.

Donna You're telling me, it took me fifteen minutes to get across the car park.

Julia I hadn't realized you would find entering the reception area such an ordeal.

Donna I wasn't scared. I just got my heel stuck in the tarmac.

Julia Of course you did.

Fiona My mum had a friend once who got her stiletto caught in one of those grills in the floor of the shopping centre.

Blanche How terrifying for her. To be trapped like that, inside a shopping centre of all places. All those bright lights and the incessant chanting music, not to mention all those huge sweaty people looming towards you. The lights start to get brighter and then you suddenly realize there's no way out — just row after row of huge shoppers battering you so you can't breathe and the exit — the exit looks so far away. (*She breathes quickly and looks panicky*)

Julia Now, now, Blanche, calm down. You are perfectly safe here ...

Fiona Would you like me to play the "Tranquil Moments" tape?

Julia I think you've done quite enough already ... Just keep breathing, Blanche, you'll feel better in no time.

Fiona quickly fishes an old brown paper bag out of her rucksack and hands it to Julia who passes it to Blanche. Blanche breathes into the bag to calm her breathing during the following

Donna Lucky you brought the old bag with you.

Fiona Oh, she's marvellous in a crisis.

Cherry Sorry to interrupt, but I'm Cherry Gordon.

Fiona Oh yes, thank you Cherry, sorry to have kept you waiting. Welcome to Camp Confidence. My name's Fiona and I'm your greeter for today. This is our leader Julia who will be helping you to tackle your particular problems during this all-inclusive outdoor confidence-boosting experience.

Julia Lovely to meet you, Cherry. (*To Blanche*) Keep breathing, Blanche ... (*To Cherry*) I'm Julia Nelson ... I think we spoke on the telephone?

Cherry Oh yes, that's right.

Julia Why don't we all sit down for a moment? Get a chance to collect our thoughts. Fiona can show you to your tents after you've had a quick rest.

Donna I want to make it clear that I'm not here 'cos I've got a problem.

Fiona Oh, I thought ...

Julia It's OK Fiona, I'll deal with this. Donna, all of us here understand that you're frightened, and perhaps a little embarrassed. Nobody wants to admit that they may not be able to do things that others find perfectly natural, but that's why we are here — to help. You mustn't be ashamed.

Donna I just don't like being shut in, that's all.

Julia Who does, Donna? Who does?

Maria Blanche.

Julia Apart from Blanche.

Maria Mimi.

Julia Why don't you and I have a look around your tent, Maria. It'll be nice to get your pyjamas unpacked before tea, eh?

Maria OK ... (*She picks up her rucksack*)

Donna Your advert said it could help me.

Cherry For the price I paid, I sincerely hope that you can.

Julia Perhaps we should talk more later, Donna, after you've settled in. Fiona? Which tent has Miss Gordon been allocated?

Fiona Oh er, tent B, with Blanche. Why don't you go in and join her? She's just unpacking her bag.

Maria Maybe she should stay outside a while.

Cherry Right, I'll just get rid of this case.

Donna looks agitated

Julia Donna? You're in tent A with Maria.

Donna If it's OK with you I think I'd rather sleep out here tonight.

Julia If you would honestly feel more comfortable, then I have no objections, Donna.

Fiona Oh, but you'd be so lonely out here on your own.

Julia Not if you sleep out here too, Fiona.

Fiona But I — —

Julia You'd be giving Donna her first key to unlocking the door to her future happiness, Fiona ...

Fiona But that isn't on the schedule until tomorrow. (*During the following, she takes six plastic cups from her rucksack and places them on the tray; she then produces a bottle of wine and fills the cups*)

Julia Good, that's settled then. Now what I suggest is that we all remove our physical baggage and then meet back here at sixteen hundred hours to empty our emotional baggage.

Cherry Is that a cowpat over there?

Julia Where?

Cherry It is, isn't it ...?

Julia Really, Cherry, it's just a little clump of earth; look, I'll move it for you.

Cherry This whole field is full of mud, isn't it?

Donna What did you expect?

Cherry I hate mud.

Fiona Now, now Miss Gordon, let's not get into a flap.

Maria Aiee! You say flap — you promise you no say it again.

Donna She's off her flaming trolley.

Blanche I can't do this. I'm sorry, but I can't do this.

Julia Ladies, please! Yes, you can, Blanche.

Cherry searches through her bag and produces rubber gloves and a plastic spray gun labelled "Disinfectant"

Cherry (*spraying*) That's better ... That's it ...

Blanche I want to go home. I want to go home.

Julia No, you don't, Blanche. Cherry, please stop doing that.

Maria Oi, you no spray me with your stinking stuff!

Donna Can't you control her? She's going to destroy the ozone layer single-handed at this rate.

Cherry You're unclean, all of you — I have to protect myself.

Julia Ow, you sprayed that in my eye.

Maria She crazy woman ...

Donna Somebody take the bloody thing off her.

Blanche Oh, I hate violence. I'm going to close the flaps.

Maria You no say *flaps!*

Julia Please, ladies ... Please, please ... *Oh for God's sake will you all just shut up!*

Silence

Fiona (*moving* C *with the tray full of drinks*) Now, how's about that
welcome drink?

The Lights dim. Music plays, as if from tannoy speakers

*During the following, a camp-fire is set up. The women put their
rucksacks and bags away in the appropriate tents. Fiona takes a set
of bongo drums from her rucksack. They all (apart from Blanche,
who remains in tent B with her head stuck out) sit round the camp-
fire, Cherry between Maria and Donna*

Tannoy Announcer (*voice-over*) This is a public announcement.
The Hawaiian Brasserie will be closing at two o'clock to make
way for the planned refurbishments to the urinals. We apologize
for the inconvenience and remind guests that they are welcome to
use the sandpit (*the radio reception crackles and breaks up*) and
playground toilets situated at the rear.

The Lights come up. Late afternoon

Donna What the hell is this all about then?
Cherry I feel like I'm in the Brownies again. I hated the Brownies.
Blanche Oh dear, it's been a while since I've done any "Ging Gang
Goolie" ...
Maria You and me both, sister.

*Fiona beats on the bongo drums — the rhythm sounds like "Jingle
Bells"*

Julia What was that?
Fiona I just sort of made it up.
Donna It sounded like *Jingle Bells*.
Fiona Sorry, I couldn't find any sheet bongo music in the
library ...
Donna Oh, I dunno.

Julia Well at least it seems to have calmed us all down. Well done
Fiona and welcome, welcome to you all. Shall we link hands?
Cherry Oh, I can't ...
Donna What's wrong with my hands?
Cherry They're covered in germs.
Donna Says who?
Maria You saying I'm dirty?
Julia Let's just dispense with the linking of hands, shall we, ladies?
Perhaps we should move straight onto some introductions. Shall
we begin with you, Donna, and move round?
Donna And this is going to help me?
Julia Trust me, all you need to do is tell us a little about yourself and
what has led you here.
Donna OK ... Well, my name's Donna and I'm a single mum.
Blanche Oh, how old is your little one?
Donna Twenty-six.
Blanche Oh ... He must be a handful.
Julia Go on, Donna.
Donna OK, well, where do I start? I married a rat who left me for
a cow. My son turned into a couch potato and I fell for every snake
in the village, until I ended up on tablets. The rest, as they say, is
history.
Maria I think perhaps you have too many pills.
Julia Donna's been using metaphors, Maria.
Maria No wonder she thinks her son turned into a potato.
Julia And what did you want to achieve from this course, Donna?
Donna I want a bit of respect, self-respect that is — that's all.
Julia Thank you, Donna, you've been really brave. Now, Cherry,
are you ready to tell us why you are here?
Cherry OK ... Well, my name is Cherry. Some of you may
recognize me. I used to be an international model.

Everyone looks blank

Well, I expect you have at least heard of my husband — Freddie
Fox.
Fiona Not *the* Freddie Fox?

Cherry Yes ...

Fiona The one who tried to eat Jemima Puddleduck?

Julia Carry on, Cherry ...

Cherry Anyway, as I am sure you are all now aware, I'm a little difficult to live with. Freddie tried to tolerate my — problems, but in the end he gave up. The last I read in the papers, he was living with a newsreader in Kensington. My therapist felt coming here, with you, would be beneficial to my recovery.

Julia I do hope so, Cherry, and thank you. Now Blanche, over to you.

Blanche My story's not really so exciting. My problems began with my father. I loved him very much but nothing I ever did seemed to please him. He was too in love with my mother. I know that sounds like most children's dream, especially nowadays with all these quickie divorces, but it wasn't as good as it sounds. You see they loved each other so much, there wasn't really room for us. They used to spend a lot of time out at the pub, leaving me and my sisters alone. Mimi and I used to stick together — we had the top bedroom, you see — and so when Mimi fell ill I just sort of got used to staying in to look after her. As the years passed, and with them my dad and then my mum, I just sort of got stuck — and then I found that the thing that I wanted to do most, I couldn't do ...

Julia What was it that you would like to be able to do, Blanche?

Blanche I want to come out.

Fiona Oh, I had no idea. You poor thing.

Maria She spend too long shut up with her sister if you are asking me.

Donna Sometimes I think I may be gay.

Cherry It's actually quite fashionable at the moment.

Blanche No, I think I've been a little misunderstood ...

Julia It must have been very hard for you, growing up with the prejudices of your generation. Thank goodness those sort of prehistoric attitudes have changed.

Donna (*standing suddenly*) I feel attracted to my probation officer.

Cherry You've been in prison?

Donna Yeah, why, does it bother you?

Maria That all depends on how it is you are getting there.

Julia We are not here to judge, Maria; prejudice is a cruel and terrible gateway for angry people to walk through

Blanche But ... I'm not a you-know-what. When I said that I wanted to come out, I do, but ...

Donna (*sitting next to Blanche*) But you're scared, right?

Blanche Well yes, but — —

Julia Do you feel dirty, Blanche?

Blanche No, I mean, I'm very clean person. I sometimes wash twice a day; it helps to pass the time.

Cherry My mother said that I was dirty; she caught me in a jacuzzi with Jeremy Delderfield.

Julia That must have been a difficult situation, Cherry ...

Cherry But I wasn't being dirty with Jeremy. At least I didn't think I was — we were only kissing.

Julia And your mother found it distasteful.

Cherry She reacted terribly. I felt sick, as though what I'd done was wrong, terribly, terribly wrong. I tried not to. I tried to tell myself that the only reason Mummy was so repressed and bitter was because she and Daddy hadn't been happy.

Julia But you couldn't get your mother's words out of your mind, could you, Cherry?

Cherry No, even after I married Freddie, I still felt as if having sex was wrong.

Julia Is this how you feel, Blanche?

Blanche I keep trying to tell you — I'm not a homo sapien ...

Cherry I suppose the fear and loathing just built up inside me, until eventually they overtook my rational thoughts and became a way of life. Only it didn't suit Freddie. The stupid thing is, I love him so much — I always have.

Donna I think that's how I feel about Blanche.

Blanche But I told you, I don't have those sorts of feelings ...

Maria For someone who only goes out once every twenty years — you sure have a way with women.

Donna I was talking about Blanche Smellie (*pronounced "smiley"*) my probation officer.

Maria Blanche who?

Donna Smellie, S-M-E-L-L-I-E.

Blanche You see, I knew it wasn't me.

Maria That spells Smelly.

Donna No, it doesn't.

Maria Si, it does: S-M-E-L-L-I-E spells smelly. This woman of yours is really smelly.

Cherry I suppose it's a disorder.

Donna She doesn't smell.

Cherry I'm sorry, I was talking about my condition, not your probation officer.

Donna She doesn't have a condition.

Fiona And you thought your name was unfortunate, Blanche.

Julia Please everyone, I think we were getting somewhere; go on, Cherry.

Cherry That's why I clean everything. I don't want to but a sort of uncontrollable urge takes over me. I feel almost possessed at times.

Donna She hates being called Smelly. That's how we met; some of the other prisoners were calling her that as she walked down the hall. I don't know why but I just wanted to protect her, so I shut them up.

Maria Was this before you found out how she was spelling it?

Donna turns on Maria and grabs her by the throat

Donna I've just about had enough of you and your pathetic wisecracks.

Maria Aiee ... She go crazy — help, help me ...

Julia Come on ladies, calm down, please. I am sensing a sudden atmosphere imbalance amongst us.

Blanche Oh sorry, that'll be my bag.

Julia Donna, please let Maria go.

Donna I've dealt with bigger loudmouths than you inside and I'm not afraid to do the same out here.

Julia Donna — think of your parole, think of Blanche.

Blanche Don't drag me into it.

Julia Just let her go, Donna. Maria promises not to mention Miss Smelly again, don't you, Maria?

Donna Her name is "smiley", like Carol.
Julia Yes, of course, just put her down.

Donna thrusts Maria away

Maria By all the saints — she gonna kill me.
Julia It's all perfectly natural, Maria.
Maria Natural to kill me, you say.
Julia No, I meant this is all part of the cleansing and healing process.
  It's been a really helpful session.
Fiona Is now a good time to take orders for sandwiches?
Julia Perfect, unless there's anything else anyone would like to add.
Blanche (*sticking her head a little further out of the tent*) I've been
  having sex with my doctor. Do you think that's all right?

Black-out

*During the following, Cherry, Maria and Blanche go into their tents
and close the flaps. Donna and Fiona get into sleeping bags and lie
down. Fiona takes a towel from her rucksack and rolls it up to use
as a pillow, then places her washbag at her side*

*Julia takes a torch from her pocket and switches it on. A dim spot
comes up on her. She moves DS and produces her mobile phone. She
dials a number, struggling to see in the darkness*

Julia (*into the phone*) Roger? Roger, is that you? ... Who is this,
  please? ... Oh Toyah, I didn't expect you to answer ... Oh yes, yes
  I see. ... No — of course I don't mind. Roger always enjoys the
  theatre ... No, you mustn't be late on my account; I just wanted a
  quick word with ... Hallo ... Hallo ... Damn!

Julia exits

The Lights come up. Night

Donna sits up in her sleeping bag and lights a fag

Fiona (*sitting up*) What's the time?

Donna I didn't mean to wake you up.

Fiona Oh, you didn't; I've been awake for ages.

Donna Something on your mind?

Fiona More like something up my bum. This ground is a bit lumpy.

Donna Sorry, I know you're only out here because of me.

Fiona Oh, it's OK, I don't mind, really.

Donna I spent so long inside a prison, I just don't want to be shut in any more.

Fiona I can understand that.

Donna Can you?

Fiona Oh absolutely ... I've never actually been into a prison, but I've seen one on telly. Ronnie Barker was in there. Anyway, I shouldn't think you wanted to be locked up.

Donna No — that's true. I hated it. It was Blanche who saved me, mentally I mean. She put her faith in me and treated me with respect. Something I hadn't felt before.

Fiona I know that feeling.

Donna Do you?

Fiona Oh, yes. Rupert — that's my boyfriend — he treats me like that.

Donna Sometimes I wonder if things had been different when I was young — I mean if I'd had more of that — I may have had more confidence and I wouldn't be in this position.

Fiona Well, you certainly wouldn't be on this course.

Donna Perhaps you're right. Do you think that Blanche really has been sleeping with her doctor?

Fiona She seemed very genuine.

Donna It's completely illegal though, isn't it? Doctor sleeping with a patient. He could be struck off for that.

Fiona What, in this day and age? I thought we only did that to cats.

Donna puts out her fag and turns over. Fiona lies back down. They doze

The Lights slowly brighten and there are sounds of birdsong

Cherry emerges from her tent in rubber gloves and apron and sets to work to dust the tents and camping equipment

Blanche sticks her head out of her tent and then goes back inside again

Cherry picks up Fiona's washbag, hangs it on the washing line or airer, then continues with her dusting

Cherry (*after a few minutes*) I know you're awake. I can hear you rustling. (*She produces a bundle of wet clothing from her tent and hangs it out to dry on a line between the tents. To Blanche*) I washed out your blouse for you.

Blanche (*sticking her head out of the tent*) What for?

Cherry I thought you'd feel fresher.

Blanche In this temperature, without a blouse, what do you expect?

Cherry It's really quite nice here when nobody else is about. Why don't you come out?

Blanche I can't.

Cherry But no-one else is awake.

Blanche It doesn't make any difference.

Cherry I remember being on this modelling assignment once. It was shot on location in Barbados. We had to get up really early and walk down to the beach to catch the sun coming up. It was the most beautiful thing I think I have ever seen.

Blanche I don't think I've ever been to a beach.

Cherry Oh Blanche, that's terrible.

Blanche I've always watched life from a window.

Cherry I'm frightened of being alone.

Blanche I'm frightened of everything.

Cherry Are you really sleeping with your doctor?

Blanche Is it so hard to conceive?

Cherry Oh God, that's not what you're trying to do, is it?

Blanche No, I meant is it such an unbelievable idea, that the doctor should find me attractive?

Cherry No, of course not. Does he help you?

Blanche   He says that the patient must take the first step for themselves, like giving up smoking. You have to want to do it. He says my phobia is my way of protecting myself.

Cherry   From what?

Blanche   From life. He thinks that a phobia is something that you teach yourself to have — you're not born with them. Something, an experience or traumatic association, triggers your mind into believing that the only way you can survive is to stay away from the object of your fear.

Cherry   So, what's the answer?

Blanche   You have to teach yourself not to fear, only that's easier said than done.

Cherry   (*sitting by the tent*) I suppose, when my mother found me — us — like that, it made me feel so terrible.

Blanche   You associated sex with being unclean.

Cherry   Yes ... although it doesn't seem like that, not when I see dirt. I can't rationalize it. I just have to clean it.

Blanche   I understand. Do you miss your husband?

Cherry   Yes, do you miss your doctor?

Blanche   Not really, he only visits me for sex and I've come to the conclusion that he's not awfully good at it. I think he banks on the fact that I have nothing else to compare him with, but I have spent a lifetime reading romantic fiction. None of the men in my books want to pretend to be the gasman.

Cherry   Would you like me to clean your boots?

Blanche   Must you?

Cherry picks up one of Blanche's boots and cleans it during the following

Cherry   Do you read a lot then?

Blanche   I like poetry best.

"Closed up each chink, and with fresh bands of straw Chequer'd the green-grown thatch.

Cherry   And so she lived Through the long winter, reckless and alone ...

Blanche   In sickness she remained; and here she died.

Cherry   Last human tenant of these ruin'd walls."

Blanche I can't believe you know that.

Cherry I went out with a university student who used to read me Wordsworth constantly whilst I was on assignments. He sent me that verse after I moved in with Freddie. I think he was trying to make a point.

Blanche It reminds me of me.

Cherry Not if you change.

Blanche I think it's too late for that.

Cherry Then we're all buggered, aren't we! Now, quickly fold up your bedding roll and pass it out to me, I can give it a quick beating to shake off anything nasty.

Blanche I don't suppose I have a choice.

Cherry Thank you.

Music plays

Blanche hands out her bedding and gives it to Cherry

Cherry exits with the bedding

Blanche takes another look outside the tent, then darts back in again and closes the flaps

The music fades

Maria suddenly sticks her head out of her tent

Julia enters. She is on the phone

Julia (*into the phone*) Darling, are you there? Please call me when you get this message.

Maria darts back into her tent

Julia grabs Fiona's washbag hanging from the tent and nudges the sleeping Fiona with her toe

Fiona Oh, morning, Julia. I haven't overslept, have I?

Julia It's six thirty.

Fiona Oh, I am sorry, I didn't sleep very well. The ground was so lumpy.

Julia You seemed to be managing pretty well until I woke you up. Anyway, you had better get down to the showers quickly. Apparently, a pervert has been nicking ladies' clothing whilst they're in the cubicles so I'll need you to be on guard. (*She hands the washbag to Fiona*)

Fiona Oh, right, I'll just get my towel.

Julia I would help but I've got to make an important call.

Fiona To Roger is it?

Julia He just doesn't seem to cope well whenever I have to leave him.

Fiona He'll be missing his trout, I expect.

Julia I'll meet you back here in fifteen minutes.

Fiona stands and grabs her towel

Julia and Fiona exit

Maria opens her tent and pokes her head out. Blanche sticks her head out of her tent too

Blanche Morning.

Maria Morning.

Blanche Cherry is just dusting off my roll.

Maria Good job I wasn't hungry.

Blanche You're a long way from home, aren't you?

Maria It's not too bad; it take about an hour on the bus.

Blanche I meant Mexico.

Maria Ah, si ... Mexico. It's a long time since I see it.

Blanche You must miss it.

Maria Sometimes, si — but I miss my mother more.

Blanche Is she still there?

Maria No, she comes with me; in fact I take her everywhere I go.

Blanche Oh, how nice.

Maria You want to say hallo? (*She goes back into the tent and pops out again with a small box*)

Blanche Oh, well, I ...
Maria This is my mother — see. (*She produces a bag of ashes from the box and holds it up*)
Blanche Oh, I see ...

Cherry enters

Cherry Oh, hallo Maria, would you like me to empty that for you?
Maria You keep your hands off my family.
Cherry I'm sorry, I was only trying to help.
Donna (*waking*) Can you keep the noise down? I've got a headache.
Cherry We were only chatting.
Donna Yeah, well, I suppose you lot just aren't used to company.
Blanche And you are obviously not used to anyone who can string two syllabubs together and doesn't have a tattoo.
Cherry That's actually a pudding.
Blanche Oh, I always get those two confused.

Julia enters

Julia Good-morning, everyone. Isn't it a fabulous day?
Donna It will be when I've had a fag. (*She gets up and stretches*)
Julia You need sustenance, Donna, not nicotine. Who's for a healthy option in the cafeteria?

Nobody answers

A healthy body is the way to a healthy mind, ladies.
Cherry Couldn't you just bring us something in clingfilm?

Julia's mobile phone rings and she moves DS to answer it

During the following, Donna, Maria and Cherry put on cardigans, tidy the sleeping bags into the tents etc.

Julia Roger, is that you? ... Roger, where have you been? I've been trying to ring you for most of the night. ... Is that Toyah's

voice? ... Did she tell you that I called? ... You're what? Late?
What for this time? ... I see ... No, nothing important. I just wanted
to say ... What, tomorrow? ... OK, yes, bye ... (*She looks out front,
sad but composed, then switches off the phone, her shoulders
sagging*)

Donna (*to Julia*) Are we doing something here, or what?

Julia What? Oh right, yes. I'll be right with you. (*She takes off her
wedding ring and puts it into her pocket, turns and walks towards
the others, her back to the audience*)

The Lights fade

*Donna, Cherry, Blanche, Maria and Fiona sit down; Julia stands
to one side*

The Lights come up rapidly

Julia Now, as I was saying, we've spent a long time talking through
our problems this morning and I think it has been very productive.
However, in order to begin your rehabilitation into society we
have to practise a scenario.

Blanche I'm afraid I'm not much of a singer.

Julia It's just a bit of role-playing, Blanche. Now what I propose
is each of us acting out a little scene. If we practice everyday
situations it will help give us confidence to attempt them when we
return home. Now number one is called "The Grocer's".

Donna "The Grocer's"? When were these written, the 1950s?

Julia We can easily adapt it to "The Supermarket". Now Cherry,
you can be the shop assistant, and Maria, you can be the customer.

Maria looks around

Is there a problem, Maria?

Maria I no have a basket.

Julia This is an exercise in improvisation, Maria, you have to try
pretending.

Maria Si, I know I pretend to shop, but it don't feel right without
a basket.

Julia (*handing the peg basket to Maria*) Here, take this — will that do?

Cherry Hang on. What am I selling?

Julia You are in a supermarket.

Cherry I know, but which bit am I serving on, the deli or the bakery or the checkout?

Julia Does it really matter? Right, shall we begin, ladies?

Maria (*to Cherry*) Hallo, there, shop assistant.

Cherry Hallo, madam.

Maria I would like to buy some carrots, please.

Cherry I'm sorry, I don't have any.

Julia Can't you just pretend, Cherry?

Cherry I was on the deli counter; they don't sell carrots on the deli counter.

Julia Well, couldn't you just direct her to where she could buy carrots?

Cherry Oh, right. (*To Maria*) Why don't you try the grocer's, madam?

Maria Si, I go there. Thank you, bye-bye.

Julia Right, well done, for trying at least.

Donna I'm getting hungry.

Julia Why don't you take a turn at this, Donna? You could ask Blanche out to the cinema.

Donna If only.

Maria Excuse please, am I going to the grocers' now?

Julia No, Maria, the exercise is over.

Maria But I no have any carrots.

Donna I don't see how I can go to the cinema if Blanche won't come out of the tent.

Julia I see what you mean. How about it, Blanche; do you think that you could attempt a few minutes outside?

Blanche No, I couldn't, I just couldn't. I'm sorry. I know I'm a failure. It was stupid of me even to attempt coming on this course. I've let you all down.

Julia No, Blanche, of course you haven't.

Blanche Smellie enters, dressed in nothing but Fiona's towel, and stands behind Donna

Donna Who wants to see a poxy film anyway?

Blanche Smellie I wouldn't say no.

Donna Blanche! What are you doing here?

Blanche Smellie I'm sorry, I didn't mean to intrude. I just had to see you.

Julia Couldn't you have dressed first?

Blanche Smellie I got a call about Donna during my aerobics class so I dashed straight down here. I realized I'd look pretty stupid bursting in on you in my leotard so I went into the showers to change. Only, after I'd undressed I nipped into the loo and when I came out all my stuff was gone. The only things left hanging up in the changing room were this towel and a chicken suit.

Maria You see big bird?

Julia Calm yourself, Maria, it was only a costume. There's about as much chance of you seeing a chicken around here as somebody completing one of my course initiatives.

Fiona suddenly enters dressed in a chicken suit

Fiona Oh, Julia, you're never going to guess what happened ...

Julia Surprise me.

Maria Aieee ... It's the big bird, I get away. I go now ... Help. (*She dives into her tent, screaming*)

Julia Maria, please. It's only Fiona. Calm yourself, for goodness sake.

Fiona I'm sorry, Julia, I can explain.

Julia Let me guess. You went into the shower and when you came out somebody had stolen all your clothes.

Fiona Yes, they even took my towel.

Blanche Smellie Oh, sorry. I think that was me. I'm Blanche Smellie by the way. I came to speak with Donna.

Maria (*sticking her head out of the tent with her eyes shut*) Has it gone?

Blanche takes a small bottle of brandy from her rucksack and, leaning out of her tent as far as her shoulders, offers the bottle to Maria

Blanche I find this awfully good for shocks.

Maria opens one eye, takes the bottle and takes a large swig from it. Julia snatches the bottle and takes a large swig from it. Maria retreats into the tent. Julia takes further swigs during the following

Blanche Smellie I came here to warn you, Donna. The parole board have had a call about you.

Cherry Is Donna in trouble, Blanche?

Blanche Smellie Donna assured the parole board and me that she would be staying in a halfway house that we had found for her — didn't you Donna?

Cherry So, what's the problem?

Blanche Smellie Last week Donna didn't show up for her meeting with us and the halfway house have said that she hasn't been staying there at night.

Donna I had to be somewhere else.

Cherry I'm sure she won't do it again — will you, Donna?

Blanche And she's not moved from this spot since yesterday, I can testicle to that.

Blanche Smellie It's not that simple, I'm afraid.

Julia But if Donna's not been living in this halfway house, where has she been living?

Blanche Smellie That's what I need to know. Have you been back to your old flat, Donna?

Donna I ...

Cherry Of course she hasn't.

Fiona She wouldn't do that.

Blanche Smellie I need to know where you've been living, Donna; if you can't tell me then you leave me no choice but — —

Suddenly Blanche stands up and steps out of the tent, albeit very nervously

Blanche She's been staying with me.

Julia Blanche! What are you doing?

Blanche Is it so strange to see someone stand up for a friend?

Julia No, it's just strange to see you stand up.

Blanche I don't get out much you see and Donna helps with the shopping and things.

Blanche Smellie So, you knew Donna before coming here?

Cherry They came together, didn't you, Donna?

Fiona Oh, that's right — I remember now.

Maria (*sticking her head out of the tent, her eyes still shut*) Even though my eyes are shut. Me too, am remembering this.

Blanche Smellie (*looking directly at Julia*) Is this true?

Julia hesitates and everyone looks at her

Julia What are you all looking at me for?

Fiona (*moving to Julia*) You can help Donna, can't you, Julia? Please ...

Julia Why should I? What has she ever — — ?

Fiona *Please* ...

Julia Oh, what the hell. Yes, OK — Donna and Blanche arrived together. Satisfied?

Blanche Smellie Is it possible for me to have a look at Donna's application form? I am assuming that she would have put this new address on it.

Julia Of course, and I would have loved to have shown it to you — — (*She looks down at Fiona's rucksack*)

Fiona, understanding Julia's implication, quickly takes Donna's form from her rucksack

— but unfortunately my assistant Fiona has accidentally — — (*She looks over to Fiona*)

Fiona shoves Donna's form in her mouth

— eaten it.

Fiona (*with her mouth full*) Sorry.

Maria You should see what she do with the bongos.

Blanche Smellie OK, I get the picture — although that still doesn't explain why Donna didn't show up for our meeting.

Cherry Donna stayed to help when the doctor called this week; isn't that right, Blanche?

Blanche nods nervously

And I'm sure Blanche's doctor could be persuaded to make a statement to that effect.

Cherry and Maria get up and stand either side of Blanche

Maria You can torture us but we no say nothing.

Blanche So, I think you should stop interrogating us all now, you've got what you came for.

Blanche Smellie Is that what you think I'm doing?

Donna Well, aren't you?

Fiona Donna thought that you cared about her.

Blanche Smellie I do.

Cherry You certainly have a funny way of showing it.

Blanche Smellie Why do you think I'm here? I could lose my job for coming to find Donna today. I don't want her to go back to prison any more than you do.

Donna Really?

Blanche Smellie Really. Look, now you've explained everything and you have found yourself somewhere decent to live I'm sure I can square things, but you must keep your appointments from now on or there is nothing that I can do to protect you.

Donna I get scared, Blanche. I stood outside your office and looked up to the fifth floor and I couldn't do it.

Julia Donna's showing all the signs of acute claustrophobia.

Fiona Oh, what a nice way of putting it.

Blanche Smellie But why didn't you just tell me?

Donna What, and lose the respect of the one person who had ever shown me any before?

Blanche Smellie Donna, I think you are so brave for coming on this course. I only want to help.

Fiona And we will do anything we can to help you too.

Donna Really?

Fiona Oh yes, Julia says we need the money.

Blanche Do you think I might go back in my tent now?

Blanche Smellie Of course. Look, I had better go and ring my boss before he alerts the police.

Cherry (*taking some clothes from her rucksack and passing them to Blanche Smellie*) Here, take these, just until they find your stuff.

Fiona And don't worry about returning the towel, Rupert only uses it to rub down his ferrets.

Blanche Smellie Oh right, thank you. I'll see you next week then, Donna; I'll be waiting in the lobby ten o'clock sharp, OK?

Donna Sure, I'll be there, and thanks — for not turning me in.

Blanche Smellie Maybe we might get to go to the cinema after all, eh?

Donna Definitely.

Blanche Smellie exits

Donna Did you hear that? Blanche and I might be going to the cinema.

Julia Considering you can't even go into a tent without breaking into a sweat I wouldn't save up for the popcorn yet.

Cherry Do you have to be so negative? I thought this was supposed to be a confidence-building weekend. Look at us, we're all trying to pull together and you are the one hell-bent on undermining us.

Julia I'm sorry, it just all seems so ridiculous.

Blanche Our lives are a bit ridiculous though, really, aren't they?

Julia Not mine.

Cherry Well, lucky old you!

Blanche (*to Donna*) I meant what I said you know. You can come and live with me. The house is big enough and if you like you could sleep in the garden when it's warm — if you would feel more comfortable.

Fiona What you need is an open plan tent in case it rains.

Julia Six months of counselling and an anorak might be of more use.

Donna I don't think my budget could run to that.

Julia I'll buy you one if you like, and I'll throw in the six months counselling too, just until you can get back indoors at night.

Fiona Is that a joke?

Julia Is it so hard to believe that I would do something nice?

Fiona Yes.

Donna I don't know what to say. Thanks.

Julia Don't thank me, thank my husband; if he hadn't been having an affair with our daughter-in-law I wouldn't have the ammunition to blackmail him with.

Fiona Oh Julia, that's awful.

Cherry I'm so sorry, Julia.

Julia It's OK, I always knew it would happen one day. After all that's how Roger and I got together — whilst he was married to someone else. He seems to have a bit of a track record.

Blanche What will you do?

Julia Screw him for every penny he's got.

Fiona Couldn't you just ask him for it?

Black-out. Music blares out over the tannoy

During the following, the women retrieve their belongings and put on their coats

Tannoy Announcer (*voice-over*) This is a public announcement. We are sorry to inform you that the bingo in the main hall will not be called by our very own Chester the Chicken this evening due to a slight technical hitch.

The Lights come up and the music fades. Evening

Fiona Now, I've arranged for the minibus to wait by the main gate

Cherry I'll help you get back, Blanche, and if you like I could come over with some of my old books, perhaps give your house a quick clean or something.

Blanche That would be nice.

Cherry What will you do, Maria?

Maria I haven't been home in long time; maybe it is good opportunity to go now, bury some old ghosts.

Cherry I second that; it must be awfully unhygienic to have your mother in your handbag.

Blanche I haven't had this much excitement since Mimi swallowed a button. (*She suddenly sways*) How far did you say the bus was?

Donna Don't you worry, Blanche, I'll look after you.

Fiona Oh, I'm missing you already.

Donna grabs Blanche by the arm; Cherry holds her other arm

Julia Well, I suppose this is goodbye. I hope you are leaving with a little more confidence than you came with.

Cherry I'm happy to be a shoulder to cry on, Julia, if ever you feel like it.

Blanche Me too. I'm always in.

Julia Maybe I'll take you up on that. Good luck all of you!

Donna, Blanche, Maria and Cherry say goodbye and exit

Fiona Oh no!

Julia What is it?

Fiona I forgot to give them their certificates.

Julia I think they've surpassed our pathetic little print-outs, don't you?

Fiona Perhaps you're right. So what do we do now. Pack up?

Julia There's bingo in the hall tonight.

Fiona So I heard.

Julia What do you say to a glass of wine and a night out?

Fiona Really? I'd love it!

Julia Great. (*Rather tipsily*) Besides, I've got a business proposition to run past you.

Fiona More confidence-building weekends?

Julia I was thinking of expanding actually; there's an awful lot of unhappy ladies in this camp. I thought we could do a bit of networking tonight ... What do you say?

Fiona I say, "This will be a success, this is a success, we are a success."

Fiona and Julia laugh and exit arm in arm

BLACK-OUT

FURNITURE AND PROPERTY LIST

On stage: Two or three tents. *In Tent B*: bundle of wet clothing
Various items of camping equipment
Between Tent A and Tent B: washing line or airer. *On it*: peg basket.
Small picnic table
Chairs

Off stage: Bag. *In it*: sleeping bag, make-up bag containing compact (**Julia**)
Huge rucksack with large plastic tea tray attached. *In rucksack*: sheaf of papers, old brown paper bag, six plastic cups, bottle of wine, set of bongo drums, sleeping bag, towel, washbag (**Fiona**)
Bag. *In it*: sleeping bag, small box containing bag of ashes, cardigan (**Maria**)
Rucksack. *In it*: bedding, small bottle of brandy (**Blanche**)
Bag. *In it*: sleeping bag, cigarettes and lighter, cardigan (**Donna**)
Bag. *In it*: sleeping bag, rubber gloves, plastic spray gun labelled "Disinfectant", rubber gloves, apron, cardigan (**Cherry**)

Personal: **Julia**: mobile phone, blood sac, torch, wedding ring (worn throughout)
Fiona: handkerchief

LIGHTING PLOT

Property fitting required: camp-fire
Exterior. The same throughout

To open: General exterior lighting. Afternoon

Cue 1	**Fiona**: "Now, how's about that welcome drink?" *Dim lights*	(Page 14)
Cue 2	**Tannoy Announcer**: " … at the rear." *Bring up late afternoon exterior lighting plus camp-fire effect*	(Page 14)
Cue 3	**Blanche**: "Do you think that's all right?" *Black-out. Cut camp-fire effect*	(Page 19)
Cue 4	**Julia** switches on her torch *Bring up dim spot on **Julia***	(Page 19)
Cue 5	**Julia** exits *Cut spot on **Julia**. Bring up night-time exterior lighting*	(Page 19)
Cue 6	**Donna** and **Fiona** doze *Slowly brighten to morning effect*	(Page 20)
Cue 7	**Julia** walks us, her back to the audience *Fade lights*	(Page 26)
Cue 8	*All but **Julia** sit down; **Julia** stands to one side* *Bring up lights rapidly*	(Page 26)
Cue 9	**Fiona**: "Couldn't you just ask him for it?" *Black-out*	(Page 33)

Cue 10   **Tannoy Announcer**: "... technical hitch."   (Page 33)
            Bring up evening exterior lighting

Cue 11   **Fiona**: "' ... we are a success.'"   (Page 35)
            Black-out

EFFECTS PLOT